M

# WITHDRAWN
## UTSA LIBRARIES

# THE BUS HOME

A BREAKTHROUGH BOOK

NO. 49

# THE BUS HOME

POEMS BY

SHIRLEY BOWERS ANDERS

University of Missouri Press

Columbia, 1986

Copyright © 1986 by Shirley Bowers Anders
University of Missouri Press, Columbia, Missouri 65211
Printed and bound in the United States of America
All rights reserved

Library of Congress Cataloging-in-Publication Data
Anders, Shirley Bowers.
    The Bus Home.
    (A Breakthrough book; no. 49)
    I. Title.  II. Series.
PS3551.N344B3  1986      811'.54      85-24644
ISBN 0-8262-0603-4 (alk. paper)

∞™  This paper meets the minimum requirements of the American Na-
tional Standard for Permanence of Paper for Printed Library Materials,
Z39.48, 1984.

    "Contour Ploughing" first appeared in *Folio*, a publication of the Coy
Carpenter Library of The Bowman Gray School of Medicine. "Tobacco
Barn," "Letter to a Dead Woman," and "The Watering Place" have been
published in *Bennington Review*. "Tobacco Barn" appeared as well in *Poet
and Critic*. "Explorer" was included in *Portfolio 1984*, a publication of
Poetry Center Southeast. "Wifman" appeared in *Kansas Quarterly*; "An
Old Farmer Dies in Piedmont North Carolina," in *The Arts Journal*; "Age
Took Him Strange," in *The Crescent Review*; "Mourning Doves Walking,"
in *The Student*, the literary magazine of Wake Forest University. "Synapses"
was published in *Cumberland Poetry Review*.
    "Husband" is No. 43 in the Broadside series of Palaemon Press. It and
ten other poems in this collection appear as well in "Palaemon One," a
chapbook also published by Palaemon Press. For the chapbook and the
broadside, and for his continuing kind interest, I thank Palaemon's pub-
lisher, Stuart Wright.
    I am grateful to the North Carolina Arts Council for a grant that helped
me through the last few months of work on this manuscript. And I am
grateful to Dave Smith, teacher, friend, and gadfly.

LIBRARY
The University of Texas
at San Antonio

FOR MY PARENTS

## THE DEVINS AWARD FOR POETRY

*The Bus Home* is the 1986 winner of The Devins Award for Poetry, an annual award originally made possible by the generosity of Dr. and Mrs. Edward A. Devins of Kansas City, Missouri. Dr. Devins was President of the Kansas City Jewish Community Center and a patron of the Center's American Poets Series. Upon the death of Dr. Devins in 1974, his son, Dr. George Devins, acted to continue the Award.

Nomination for the Award is made by the University of Missouri Press from those poetry manuscripts selected by the Press for publication in a given year. George Garrett was the judge for all poetry selections made in the Press's Breakthrough Series for 1986 and 1987.

# CONTENTS

III.

IV.

# I.

Poems for James Gilmore Bowers
1888–1959

*If I forget you,*
*let my right hand forget her cunning.*
*If I do not remember you,*
*let my tongue cleave*
*to the roof of my mouth.*

## 1. My Father Never Got to Russia

He was a man who never changed his mind.
But someone told me: young and burly,
full of the daily endless railroad run,
full of the harridan dependent mother,
expensive sisters, one brother dead
of railroad cars, another gone
with drink, bung full
of sisters' husbands, Jesus!
Daddy left, for Murmansk, Leningrad,
wherever all that clacking track
the old czar laid down with his ruler
cut the steppes in half. Lincoln Steffens
said the future worked there.
He meant to see it.

Got just as far as New York City.
Next thing anybody knew,
here was Big Bull-Necked Gilly back again
among the ties. Nobody ever learned
what turned him round
and coaxed him home to all the yokes.

## 2. Sweatband Poem

Home from the train on Sunday
and no churchgoer, he wore his old felt hat
jammed to the eyebrows,
clean bib overalls, silk socks,
high-button work shoes already out-of-date.
He sat on the porch. Picture it:
1940, a righteous socialist,
feet to banister, straight chair tipped
to the stretch of his legs, his rare leisure.
When my brother wired that chair,
when he hid round the corner
with the hand-cranked generator Daddy saved
for Christmas lights, when my brother
ground the current out,
its whirr shot our father godless,
harmless, stung, swearing by nothing
through his house. Dadblame,
he hollered, running in railroad shoes,
chasing the child whose science
turned him to a lightning rod.

## 3. At the Slaughter

It seems that at his best he thought
*consequences: require no more*
*than I can face.* He was principled,
he was a meat-eater;
those things I remember. About the other,
they tell me he went innocent
to the shambles, to see for himself.
He watched the great sledgehammer smash
the calf's skull, its body half die
in that crush, eye burst from brain,
two quick legs scrabble in blood, quiver,
grow quiet. They say he crept home.
I know he ate no more veal
or lamb, no young meat, irrationally, ever.

## 4. His Hand

Before he met Mama, his right hand
was down to three digits.
Nosy as any other child, I knew
every pit on the butt of that ring finger.
He told me when I asked:
crushed in a coupling, boxcar, caboose;
careless, he said; once he knew her,
he took more pains. That big maimed hand,
deft, could not be less than rough.

## 5. 1939

You planned the stop to let the radiator rest
at a scenic overlook, where you wrapped twine
around a watermelon,
tapped through rind,
squeezed through the pulp.
I see your hands pull the string tight
through its lessening circle,
earth soak up the sweet red water
running from the cleft, sweet water
that dried sticky
on the old car's running board.
I see hands pass chunks of melon
while the engine cools.

Surely you told us how it was
that string cut fruit. You were big
on facts. But I don't remember.

Another time: lights strung sleepy
over the Ashley. I see a head—where
is your face?—shaped blank against night,
against the same old car's interior, scratchy
dun plush. One hand, a steering wheel,
lights strung beyond a windshield, the night sky:
nothing more of Charleston; nothing of you.

The one film you liked, a fairy tale.
In the fright-gulping great dark room
among gnomes sobbing and glass-casketed
death, I feel your hand swallow mine,
remember it, not you, not you then.

Baffled, I sift for bits
to build an image in your blind spot.

## 6. His Intelligence, Our Education

From cinder dirt by railroad sidings,
from low land near the boarding house
at the far end of his run,
he dug wildflowers:
two kinds of jewelweed,
columbine, wild geranium, sundrop,
trillium, star jasmine.

From somewhere he brought home
for us to learn them
plaques of different woods,
veneer chips of the various oaks, maples;
yellow poplar, no true poplar, but the tulip tree,
he was careful we should know that;
pines, so many; ash;
plaques slung on string like paint-hue samples;
I remember their textures, their dry odors; cedar;
I remember names, but would not know the woods;
what did we learn? Not what he taught.

He brought home rocks.
Clusters of quartz crystals. Mica, in sheets.
Bauxite by the lump: white streak in red sponge.
Bauxite powder smooth from the mill's battering,
so we could see what happened to it.
Fool's gold, and the real thing in its ore,
blue vein through pudding stone.

We sunk the wildflower roots in the back garden
by the black walnut's trunk.
The wood chips lay in his glass-front bookcase
with *Ten Days That Shook the World*.
Those rocks stayed on the fancy tray on the sideboard
(a wedding gift, dead butterflies and milkweed tassels
rotting under glass edged with twisted raffia) for years.

## 7. Memorial Day Weekend, 1943

Still wearing his conductor's hat,
hot with virtue after half his run,
his train in on time, due home tomorrow,
he pitched right from the rocker
to the boardinghouse veranda floor,
lay there till they moved him
to the parlor sofa. He waked,
talky, through night-train coupling noises,
steam emissions, whistle shrieks.
They hauled him back like freight.
That road ran by his track.
Braced for the effort, he sat high
in the swaying ambulance, eyes avid at the window
for cinder banks, for the passing train,
for wild geraniums pushing pink and weak
through soot. Insistent, he talked, fluent.

Home, they carried him to bed.
He said "I'll walk." They said "No."
He slept that night.

He lay still for the doctor, heard his wife:
"They called me all the way to Wadesboro.
But it's not so bad. See,
it's not so bad. He's better.
Aren't you better, Gilly?"
He heard the answer, "Bed rest,"
heard his wife say "Thank you," listened

as, talking, they left the silent patient

poking the plates and crevices
of his skull, peeping through gelatin,
weighted, tongue gone to stone
between night and that morning.

## 8. Dumb Love

We're lucky there's a war, Gilly.
With all these shortages, nobody
else can buy much either, nobody
has to know we're bad off.

Eyes blinked in his head.

I'm going to sell the car, Gilly.
I won't drive,
you won't be able to.

He shifted his weight, drew in
the numb right foot, the clumsy hand.

The spare tire's already gone, Gilly.
I rolled it to the filling station
you traded at.
They bought it.
We have to eat.

He said Yes.

I'll read you the funny papers.
I'll read you the death notices,
the *National Geographic*. You'll like that,
Gilly. We'll manage.

Oh, he said. Oh.

## 9. Burke Street

After the damage, Daddy rambled Burke Street,
fruit sack bulging with staples
on shoulder, never again to be caught
short: salt, bread, toilet paper.
I lagged, wanting not to be known
to know him, going his direction, known.

17

## 10. Service for the Dead

*for my father*

He's dying finally, the voice says.
I hang up the phone, turn from the friend
in my bed. It's time to go.

Now, in the dark, I remember
his pacing sleepless when the foot cramps hit,
how I waked through dead-end child nights
while he shoved his pillow in his mouth,
sobbing for losing something; my mother surely
could not have slept, still in her bed
beyond the table from him.

Almost morning. In the airport coffee shop
another isolate shakes pellets
from a bottle. B-1. Its odor stuffs
my nostrils, my throat fills
with the saliva that comes before vomit,
and I remember: the home remedy
against diabetes. That odor—
there is none like it—surged from the bottle
like a bubble from a child's soap pipe,
like speech ballooning
from a comic mouth. His own speech
fought in his mouth,
perverse, words, when they came,
clotted; ideas crumbled at his lip.

I buy a candy bar. He had a taste
for sweets. Sugar became present
in all his secretions. His saliva
reminded him of his sins of appetite,
urine dried sticky on the toilet seat.

I climb the rolling stair to the plane's
body, hand on guardrail, the smelted metal
cold from night, wet from dew. My hand
takes it all in, water, weather, metal.
I pocket my hand, think how
once at the farm, set to keep an eye on him,
I kept my distance,
watched him wander the perimeter
of the pasture, peer for bearings,
grasp the hot fence. Nothing worked
its way to his sense, not my gasp, my laugh,
the quick shock from the wire. He moved off.
I thought "Now he's a nonconductor."
I am in the plane, hands wrapped
on coffee cup, ready for the next step.

I find him dying on his bed, his eyes
dull with cataract. Pain leaks from the stump
of his foot. "Hurts," he grunts,
as we turn him. "It's all right," we coo.
"Not all right. Not all right. Wait."
We cannot wait. We have waited
too long. His grunts do not
by one jot mitigate our mercy.
Does he know I am here? I push my face
to the skin of his forehead. He mumbles "Who? Who?"

## 11. A Souvenir from a Visit to the City

Your Russian peasant jumping jack is antique
now, in his red slouch cap, gold tunic,
wood britches with their carved stylized folds.
His beard juts springy as ever,
his hands, palms out in the priest's
gesture of blessing, jiggle, lift, drop;
his boots kick like any other
jumping jack's. You bought him new
in New York City. Did you say
he is Ukrainian? Do I imagine that?
How did you know? He hangs from a pin
in your granddaughter's bedroom.
When he needed new strings, I matched
the old knots, precisely. You would be proud.
He makes your great-grandson laugh.

## 12. Easter Saturday, City Cemetery, Winston-Salem, North Carolina

We scrub the stones, ready
for another Easter, my daughter,
my grandson, and I, with no clear notion
why we do this thing. Nicholas, who is small
and tires soon of any amusement, washes slapdash
at the smallest grave, under the forsythia border,
an infant second cousin. With an ice pick
my daughter digs soot from the letters
of my father's mother's name. I tend my father.

This bird-dropping stain is green verging to plum.
I wonder what the minerals are,
what chemicals, how they combined
to make these colors I bleach out.
I have no sense of dirt.
Detergent foam from my brush bristles
runs white into the mud that is red
from iron in our soil. I see the soil
suck moisture, trace of foam
alter the earth it enters.

We are done here and my grandson is restless.

I gather our tools.

To whom do we minister? Our dead
were ready, I think. These motions we make
not for them, people beyond being people,
beyond needing anything. Not one wanted
a last wish. Not yet beyond anything, I wish
for them to be allowed not to rise,
not to rise, to be leached
free of all they were, in their integrity
held steady, like ducks in a press, under clean stones.

I turn to the car. Nicholas must be carried;
his mother wears him on her shoulder,
whispers to him. The easy freight
of the bucket swings by its bail
from her free hand. Glancing back,
I see her lean into the wind
as the bucket swings, as she follows, as her son dozes.

# II.

## Tobacco Barn

Always a place of business even swept clean,
empty, cold, October through June it reeked
of seared sweet leaf that grabbed
the nasal membrane. Then in summer
his tobacco barn took on its purpose,
stood at the first priming full
as a rain forest, cool green racked swags
of leaves rising to the ridgepole. If next day
he took you in, curious, inching across
the hot red dust, you found leaves curling
like sunburn under the old wood-burning furnace's
heat, one-twenty-five Fahrenheit caving the skin
in moon-crater pocks you thought sure
would show later, the pressure was that heavy.

Tobacco's a consuming thing, with no time off
for thought backward, forward, lateral:
regret, hope, responsibility: just the simple
dense sensation, and that's what got him,
spring after spring in the plant beds, then
to the lean-to shed against the barn
deep among pine and redbud
where his old cot sagged, full of bugs, years
after his last priming. This was no mystery.
And he had help; he and his hands
took turnabout, stoking the stove around the clock
till the last leaf cured out sweet as honey.

Someone may build on that, the juxtaposition,
sweet malignant weed, body. But what else
in western North Carolina could he have done?
The facts were there, and he used what he had:
trees, barn, leaf, hands, heat, bed.

## An Old Farmer Dies
## in Piedmont North Carolina

Since she died, my burying clothes
is ready too, and they had better
put me in them when I go.
I buried Mama white like what she wanted,
and I am ready here inside, and if
my nieces knowed I know they're there,
why, I could tell them one more time
to put them on me, all the white
and unworn starchy clothes
that I've laid waiting ready.

I won't wear a necktie.
I never did love neckties.
Whenever there was burying I had to wear a necktie,
but I'll not do it this time,
and if they want me shaved and clean,
they's one of them must do it, for I'll not.

But my clothes is clean.
White overalls.
A fine white shirt and socks.
I've wore no socks but white ones since the doctors
cut on me and taken that big wart
out from my heel, but these white socks is different,
fine white socks. And underwear, two suits,
one summer, one good heavy winter weight.
For I'll be ready, whatever time
of year I go; now it's fall; I don't know
which they'll choose to put me in.
I don't know which they'll choose to put me in.

I'll lie by Mama in my white.
I buried her in white like what she wanted,
all those years when we was two alone.
Her I married late
I buried early, in the blue
she wanted; I done right by her, she's
with her people;
and I'd not have needed no one else
had Mama lived. She knowed
I love my Jesus. Mama knowed I love my Jesus.

When I come to her, with a fine white hound
and mule, all in my white,
she'll know me, and we'll farm
a hill again, with one cow, just one
milk-white heifer, that will give her milk
to Mama. And the milk will foam.

## Age Took Him Strange

You know, her relict puttered
around after she died
for years and years. We learned
what rheum was, watching
his eyes. He lived thin
longer than anybody thought
he would, squat,
there in the settling dust,
waiting for nothing,
while the trace of her
flaked off, no matter
how he husbanded it.
When the corruption
got him, when his brain leaked
with the other stuff
out from those pink lids, then—
wonder! his flesh rose. In one
antique flourish, he groped for women
like an old dog running asleep,
then dropped sticky into the silence
she had ready for him
like she always did
his morning breakfast.

# Wīfman

*Wīf* is itself from A. S. *wīfan*, to join, to weave, and refers (probably) not to the *wife's* being linked to her husband, but to the usual occupation of the female department of the household. Baking and weaving: weaving is preserved in *woman*; baking, in *lady*.

—*Dictionary of Word Origins*, ed. Joseph T. Shipley

The old loom smacked, weft
grew under the shuttle
flying side to side, as she sat
humped and diligent,
settler of no place
commonly thought frontier.
She wove plain cloth.
She had nine children.
She had one house slave;
admit it; a wedding gift;
this was the South.
The war had passed. Still
she knew her duty, would not
turn off another working woman.

So she wove coarse cloth, tough
fabric good for lying on,
for wrapping babies in; a comfort.

Her sons went raw to the fields,
daughters mastered at five
the gutting of chickens,
at eight their throttling, vanished
mute and knowing into marriage.
They stayed thin till, like her,
they went slack with bearing.

The old loom smacked in the loft,
shot dust motes spinning
in particular frenzies
into light beams runneled through chinks
where dry mud fell from the daub.
Cloth grew, the color of wheat flour.
She sheeted the dead. Her slave
friend died. The shroud
was their best unbleached domestic.
No waste, she said.
"She done earned it. She was
a good hand to work.
We was like to one another
as two peas from a purple hull."

She fell sick late, lay
on the old bed-ticking stuffed with husks,
remembering lyings-in. She drenched
the sheets, muttered "Shame
to do them this way." She sucked dust.

She heard in each indifferent thump
the loom's slam, saw in hearth glimmer
summer morning light, shearing gloom.
She dreamed the loft. "We done good work."
Dim in her vision inched a billow,
cloth from the machine she crawled
like a scaffold underpinning, treadle
to hanger. She clung limp
to a breaking warp thread.
Her dream-cloth spread wide,
cornering the cold sky, blotting
stars that had hung thick.

As the cloth dropped, she smiled.
"Good weaving," she thought she said.

## Her Memory of Early Winter

Washbowl: clay with white glaze
on the white stand. Water
under a membrane of crystals.
The lace curtain blown aside,
cool to the hand; cold air,
the windowsill, its blunt curve,
its raised sash beside the bed.
Snow granular on her pillow slip,
pricking her cheek as they waked.
These she remembers. Mornings.
How the sisters shared
that sleepy chill.

Old and insular, she fingers
white tatting
edging old linen, old consciousness
swimming against the stream:
widowhood, births, marriages,
merging in the single, sisterly
and distant, beckoning cold.

# Explorer

*And he stayed yet other seven days;*
*and sent forth the dove; which returned*
*not again unto him any more.*

—*Genesis 8:12*

She was fastidious, would not rest
her foot on carrion. The raven had.
That first time, exhaustion brought her back.
One week later it was duty,
bearing one leaf from the limb that beckoned,
branched enough to hold one bird.
Hard to leave that perch. Hard to return.

In the clamorous Ark another week
her dove brain craved solitude,
nestlings crowding
the indifferent accommodating breast.
She comforted her male,
wind shrilling in her ear
past tree bones jutting
from glutted mudpools.
She listened for its hiss,
answered the third time
Noah tossed her into emptiness.

## She Speaks from the Desert

It's hard to remember him.
Coming here was my idea too.

Looking at mesquite.
This time of year at home
dogwood would bloom.
There would be trailing arbutus.
Sourwood comes later, small
and white in summer. Bees notice.
I miss that honey.

## Saving the Apples

Scattered on the property were old apple trees. Nobody we knew planted them. That kind of tree will bear as long as it has sap, but the fruit is small, not much larger than its own core, misshapen from insect damage, hard. Nobody bothered to pick those apples. Even when they fell for us, we let most rot; of those we raked up, the bulk went to the pigs. Still that left bushels of fruit the size and shape of thumb joints. That fruit she pared, then sliced close to the seed, spread on stretched cheesecloth on the back porch. When they were shrunk to the texture and resilience of shoe tongues, she bagged the slices in muslin pouches, hung them in the pantry off the porch. All winter and into spring those slices went to applesauce, turnovers, hypocrite pie—thick apple paste buried in custard. The odor of apples soaked the raw wood walls, infused each splinter with the essence of a chip of fruit.

# The Ancillary Woman

After she died, her nieces cleared
away the paper scraps disjunct
and immaterial as the bits of satin
she did not make into comforters.

They found a Kodak photograph:
four children, pine tree: 1910.
Younger sister's hair in streaks
across the face, a screen
against annoyance in the static eyes
and mouth. One brother squatting
skinny-calved in cotton drawers,
hair summer-fever-short, shrinking
into Big Sister's skirt—she fixed
at thirteen; she, too, squinting
into sunlight, baby brother in the lap.

One other picture: 1945: Big Sister
indentured to the others' apples, tough
and knobby windfalls pared, cored, sliced, dried,
sacked to hang through winter.
She is turned three-quarters to the camera,
no time to pose, but smiling, hands
sunk deep in pyramids of apple slices,
cupped hands lifting double cuddled heaps
of slices sliding off the heap, tumbling
like plenty past the drawstring.

This her servitude, her
offertory: not her apples.

## Aunt Nell's Cooking Things

I have some of the knives,
soupspoons, serving spoons;
I have her blue glass measuring bowl.
It lasts. Bowl, not cup,
lipped for pouring, thin,
but not a chip is gone.
I love the lip and gripping
edge, the feel of glass, like scooped bone,
polished thin with emptying.


## Contour Ploughing

Following the ploughshare's tough
and abnegatory, but its edge,
when you don't force it,
seeks the shape earth's easy with;
mule knows that path,
finds it for you, stubborn;
let mule and blade go on,
they'll turn soil and stubble,
tug rock, dislodge
old dead roots;
all you have to do's
hang on tight, trust the plough,
make yielding seem natural.

# III.

## Mourning Doves Walking

Two grave doves walk the lawn, down
between two buildings,
under one black tire swung vacant
in the late-day sun,
to two white oaks
green in a glancing light
with sooted trunks, ridged, dove-
grey. The doves move,
dipping, beyond, to deep grass,
lush, where the mower missed,
then go. They leave no wake, no track,
on concrete, on dirt flattened
beneath the tire, on grass.
Their slight weight on earth
traces no thing, as they breast the light
that seals behind them
as their feathers sheathe.
I see their fine progress,
wish, engrossed, to leave
no evidence, not even that
of vacancy, to move off
with the light gravity of doves.

# The Watering Place

## 1.

Kudzu sprawls the ravine, drapes
the trees it chokes
where hovels skewed at the sinkhole brink, where kudzu
stood at bay
when I was a girl. Now it claims
each artifact.
Lizards skim stems, make no quiver in the least.
Snakes run here
for creekbed holes, and clay waits gray and cool
with iron-red streaks.
These are the rank bleak colors and beasts I know
no others like.
Heat wells from the pond bottom to seethe
everything, and
kudzu leaves blaze. Their spirits rise
in a quake
of sun-deluded air. I stand
roped calf-deep
in a prodigal and aimless vine.

## 2.

I crept here just one time, against all the rules,
where boys clung
mother-naked on kudzu trailers braided for strength
and slung from tree crowns,
those great braids flipping boys who gripped them
in arrogant groins
then fell like mites to dimple the pond with their spill
while the vine,
bound to its purpose, swung through the arc prescribed
and came to rest
plumb and grave, true as a compass needle.

That was what I saw as, white and strange
to the pond life,
I lay heavy on clay that smudged an iron stain
into my skirt.

3.

The time I fumbled the question out—"May I
go swimming too?"
—they said, "Why, that place sunk in brush beyond
    shacktown,
buried in kudzu,
that red-mud cleft filled with soiled water, that sinkhole,
that is no place for a girl."

Why would a girl want to go there? Any good girl?
To learn what boys learned
together, where foam gathered white on red-brown
    waste water
welling up in the gully?
I wanted to swim. It was that simple. To hug kudzu,
depend on it,
drop weak off and fall back to the water, streaked
abdomen and
between the breasts and legs with its smear.
And had not
one word for the ache, to feel, to be.

4.

I watched kudzu take the trees
the young men
fell from. Dumb and puzzled, graceless, they tumbled
out of the air,
crept from water. They worked the red dirt, stepped
to their fathers' gait,
hacked the vine back to its root.
They drained the sump.
Red dust caked their tongues. Sun

baked their necks.
Their thumb skin cracked. Their young eyes
went deader
than lizards', snakes'. They grinned to remember
the old swimming hole.
And while they grinned, the vine inched its tips
under their boot-soles.

5.

Too late now for the sinkhole, I will
my way back
to the kudzu jungle, wait hot in its itch.
Dead boys swing
out on dry vines. I know
their eyes, I share their nightmare,
"let the surface
be soft, let us be welcome,"
always a plea
like the refrain of a child's horror story.
The pond lies filmed.
One lizard rears its blunt self, eye slit viscous.
When they strike,
when the tension gives, I celebrate
the foreign bodies, all
pimples, tumors, boils, bred by this body
like a swamp
I lie inside and cry from. The cry
is left. It ties me
to the dirt I love where kudzu crawls in the heat,
snakes run, pond water works its deep way
through malleable red clay to root.

# The Clay-Handler

I remembered him dumb as the rest of us
were dumb, but special.
So when he turned potter,
firing the clay
till it burned white and brittle,
what else was likely,
given the time lost? I went looking
for his work, bought one vase
that narrowed up from bell to neck,
smooth-lipped, glazed outside
the various greens of kudzu.
Its white throat opened a thumb's width,
enough for two stems of kudzu blossom,
purple, a plain flower, easy to miss. Later,
when he quit the wheel, what did it matter?
The vase broke, and he never knew I had it, anyway.

# Letter to a Dead Woman

*Sylvia Plath, 1932–1963*

Two years' difference wouldn't matter now.
Even young we would have noticed
what we had in common: anger,
waste intelligence, pride;
once in a while, a shock.
New York. That city would eat anybody.
Coupling without conviction, for the wrong reasons.
The craze to marry. And then children.

Of course I managed. But lately I think of you,
balance your truncated clear screech
and my endurance.
You know which comes up short.
I'd like to see you fifty, with pearls, bleached.
The last man I'll make love to had gray pubic hair.

# Husband

I wouldn't lie to you.
You weren't safe with truth,
you'd turn it sideways and cut with it.

All you left possible was silence.
What I didn't say was nothing
you suspected—you knew
how wrong you were—
but the occasional good thing.
I'm sorry you never knew about your grandson.
Your last letter: obscene rhymed couplets:
I thought it canceled my last debt.
Did I owe you another offer, any fact?

Dead one year to the day when I found out.
The never less-than-daily fear:
*when will he turn up, when will I have to speak*
*again to his crazy meanness?*
*The poor beat bastard*
*will be ugly to deal with,*
*but there'll be help he'll have to have,*
*and I'll have to give it.*

Mean comes before crazy, I used to think.

Houston. What a place for you to die,
where the freeway interchanges loop and loop
like earthworms copulating.
I imagine you, cracked feet bare,
all your teeth gone,
dressed by choice in the dirt of Houston
and the redundant coverall
they forced on you when you got stopped
on a side road, one last time nude,
no ID, money thrown away.

I imagine you loose in a hideous late night,
racing, racing the freeway, shoulder to median,
looking for the safe place,
dodging the loving vehicles
till one lucky one caught you.

I wish you had not lain in the morgue unclaimed.
Your grandson is healthy.
It is good to know you are dead.

Synapses

I.

The coffee-brown girl claimed by her seizure
at Liberty and Fourth, at the green lamppost
where I leaned, early, after the night's work,
waiting for any bus home—
lamppost her head rang on like a clapper
as she reached snapping for it or me when she sank—
that girl's lips more than her eyes stay with me,
thick and yielding smile.

The girl drooped, bent
breast-high to me now, and I buckled
to gather her, face in the scoop of my neck,
my right hand dug in her glistening hair
to hold the whipping head away
from hard surfaces; then swung, a cradle for her,
down to the granite curb.

She thrashed remote in the pavement dust,
all body. I crouched
at her shoulders. Other dumb hand forced
other parts. A mutter: "Hold her knees."

Sun flashed from a watch-crystal. Its quick glare
blanked my hand cupping her cheek
as she swam back to herself, wordless. I said
"You'll need ice for that knot on your forehead."
Her grave lips curved, an admission.
That grave curve, puffed, welts my brain,
scar of an old lesion.

II.

Home to my daughter's leavings, and to certain fears—
Is she in school? Did she pack a good lunch?
How much can I stand?—kicking aside the clutter

47

ditched in her battle,
the usual struggle.
I drift into the day's thin sleep,

roused in minutes by women below the window,
their raw mouths dripping. "I know better
than to believe what any kid says."
"Nothing a girl that age can do
to surprise me." "We all got through it,
they will too." "See them swimming,
you'll know they ain't babies any more."

When my child and I swam, seeing her breast,
pride in her long back, were my permissible joys.
Eyes open under water, we let ourselves surface,
shattering the bright planes, breaking the tension
near where her friends waited.

My eyes are deserts. Muscles tug at me
with one spasm. I think "A myoclonic jerk,"
the idea a disjuncture. I've got to rest.
Sacked as a city, I lie
open to pillage, thinking:

the girl, my girl, knotted in herself,
the rigor of her grief,
lip gripped against the sob
that shudders out, a convulsive tremor,
one torn gasp. Shocked, she has no word for her loss
in the gibbering normal bargain.
Tongue-tied, I say "That lip will be swollen,
the way you're biting it. Don't cry so hard."

She came perfect, shapeless.
They're right, the women: the twisting nightmare
ends in the hard second birth
that will leave her maimed and formed.
I want to say "I stood it. I promise
it will never be worse than this.
Look at me." I see her flinch, and I sleep.

III.

In her kindness, a friend asks
"What did you need it for?
You seem OK to me."

*The jellied smear in the hair. Electrodes at temples,*
*straps, formal protective ranked shy henchmen*
*guarding the joints. Why is the one at left*
*familiar, why is his image clear?*
*Crossed hand cupped, bracing the kneecap,*
*he smiles, embarrassed. An acquaintance.*
*One white snap, brain a drumhead rapped*
*once, smartly. The gradual surfacing,*
*residual muscle ache. Smoothing the skin back on.*

If I have an answer, it is
I was young, there were people
who thought it might help.

IV.

In the craving for a balancing joy,
what is there to settle for,
walking gingerly, like Agag, among electrical
    malfunction,
the sexual function and its early swindle,
any social dysfunction? The bus home
is a long time coming,
the craving for joy and balance
longer. I have no sure word for my daughters,
high-breasted, long-backed, various-hued,
driven to earth, but that the choices,
if pointless, are a common lot:
quick epileptic glitter, occasional
indifferent shock, grave smile,
the rank comfort of work.

# The Bus Home

Somewhere on the way back
in the dark between Richmond and Lynchburg,
in the smelly Greyhound air-conditioned chill
slick and stale as cheap hair oil,
a stranger will astonish you,
smiling, spreading his jacket over
your shoulders, your cold upper arms,
as you lie—invisible, you thought—
in the corner of window and rough seat back.

You will know but will not trust for years:
something in your condition touched him.

You will sleep better, warmly. Sleep
is what you need as you are driven
back to what you ran from.

Starting from the Port Authority terminal,
somehow through New Jersey. Then
the long black stretch south
from State Road Delaware with its cafeteria
where you ate lime jello. You roused
at Washington. Between gluey eyelids,
through tinted glass, you glimpsed
the tumescent Capitol and the Monument rising
lime-green, livid as neon beyond
your nearer vision, accidents
of wreckage. Borne on down the road
you doze, happy when you sleep, Fortune's
child. Doomed one, blessed one. Not
till you have finished failing may you prophesy.

Twins

Sharing and lacking certain parts,
you puzzle from the start
at the simplest acts:
breathing, walking, the excretory
and sexual functions.

Perhaps without a scalp,
no fontanel for either, your skulls
open like mouths, the cerebral membranes
intimate as palms, you lie fixed
lengthwise. Your first sight
of your two selves, known
and not wondrous,
will come later, mirrored. If you walk,
you will be a shaky omega, that last thing
unstable but inexorably coming on.

Or you are less: infants, close,
one head rising serious
from the mutual trunk, taking shelter
in the curve of the other's shoulder,
facing the soft neck. Her lips flutter
to the insufficient lungs' struggle, brush
the sister's neck skin, form an involuntary,
hoping O; such union! Her eyes are closed.
You two will not last long.

You may be joined at the groin,
your torsos superior, distorted, at right angles
at the single shapeless pelvis
above the organs and the legs, two, three, four,
scrabbling in their different lengths
for something to stand on.

Some have no flesh belt,
like Eng and Chang's, that got stretched
and leathery with age,
but come into the singular world
discrete, in clear pairs,
matched for all to see,
with worried eyes searching
till your glances enter one another
and you are full. In your subtle
likeness, born from experience
arrogant and double-sure, each knows
of the other "He is my twin.
Nobody else is good enough."

No body else. You are closest of all
who have no apparent tie, no known
kinship, not even proximity, just
an unlikely joyful creed:
    *I will never find him. He is*
    *no less there. Face and sex*
    *irrelevant, he is no less my twin.*
You are most one, invisibly, when
whatever the severance—flesh, blood,
space, time, monstrous shortcoming,
ugly violent division—when, separate,
you lurch away apart
as we do now; as you always must.

# IV.

# A Partial Geography of North Carolina: The Northwest Piedmont

1.

From my bell-tower office
four levels up, I watch the weather
come over the mountains, cloudbase breached
and gushing like any bag of water; I watch
the weather master the skyline, see it tumble
like surf over the near monadnocks
and the more distant Blue Ridge.

                         When I turn
from one steeple window to another
ninety degrees north, my range of vision
broadens, my own irregular dimpled view
here in the late afternoon
that, high and dry, I watch
on borrowed or stolen time.
But I have to work at it. I crane
to see past the chin-high windowsill.
To see those old hills, even to bring
my eyes to peep level, I must stretch my neck
long as a reptile's.

                Rain is on the way.
I wait out the era
and take bearings without compass, sextant,
even astrolabe. It's a good thing
I am alone today, watching the weather.

Ours comes from the north,
usually, historically. Patrick Henry knew it
as metaphor. When he said, "The next gale
that sweeps from the north," people understood
the implication. What's new
in weather as a metaphor? Nothing
I have to tell you.

And this storm
comes at me out of Henry country, country
of Jefferson, of Light-Horse Harry
Lee, all those other Lees,
all those productive fathers.
This was never pilgrim country,
justification never was their first
illusion. They knew what was what:
merchandise, merchandise, merchandise;
they knew what they were after
in their revolutions,
for good or ill, those Lees and Henrys.
But coming straight from their country,
straight from the heart
of Virginia, Daddy didn't, except the two
he thought better of—against family,
against profit. He thought better
of his revolutions. What was his merchandise?

Country of all those productive
fathers, and mine. He grew his own religion,
thought he was godless, the old man

who, young, came down those valleys
like the train he conducted,
cumbered with baggage:
brood abandoned in his own father's
declaration of independence: siblings,
the squat mother yelling at her drone
"Go! Go! Gilly's a man, he'll take care of us!"

                          Seventeen.
He learned his "no" well. "No," he said
to the other, the parent who pleaded
"Come with me," who offered "Come with me."

There comes the rain, sure enough,
down from the northwest, working
its dog-leg way through the trough
that runs southeast by Sauratown
and skirts the old Pilot, humped mass
settling into Stokes County well east
of the rest of its range.

The Pilot must have made a racket
when it shot off the last time,
whenever that was, big hill blowing
its lid plumb off so the pinnacle
sits askew forever beside the hollow cockpit
of its crater. Foxed by distance,
time, familiarity, I see the silhouette
soft in the rain, the pinnacle
an ovate form topped by a frieze of pines
winter, space, and rain make look like fur
sprouted above the drop of its sides,
rumpled by some big friendly hand.
Deceptive. I know those rockfaces,
how they claim foolish hikers,
know the tall pines, how they
supplant one another.

These are my views to the northwest.

2.

Beside the west window
I've tacked an old photo, a picnic.
Sometime before 1938 it must have been,
for Grandma Bowers is there, sunk
in the middle of the old whole family;
quilt for ground cloth, food.
One plum has rolled to the quilt's edge,
lies half split, its pit peeping
between the halves; in the background,

the rope catwalk slung across the Pilot's crater
to the knob, and that rickety ladder
up the rockface stern as the family
faces at the communal quilt; were we
having fun? Did someone climb that ladder
up to the rocky knob? My sister, heavy
adolescent, my skinny brother?
What was there to be found?

Ladder and catwalk are long since down,
and Pilot's a public place now.
Since she travels faster, since
she grew up, my daughter goes there
with friends, to watch sunsets, is home
not long after moonrise; Pilot Mountain's
no more than a suburb, what with the superhighway
and the good broad paved secondary road
running clear to the summit.
Whatever mystery was there is gone
with the risk, but there still seems
to be pleasure in the place.

How do they know themselves?
What will their direction be?
    *Down the broad way do I go.*

There sits Grandma in the photo, solid
as the Pilot's knob and blinking
through steel-rimmed spectacles,
eyelids like window shades, fine pink skin
and white hair under her straw hat, honored
whether she had it coming or not, alone
among her kin, that wealth of family.
They say she lit out, young,
on a line straight as a surveyor's,
Bluefield down to Bristol,

bit in her teeth,
kicked over the traces,
headstrong. She who destroys:
the rebel, Grandpa in tow raw and grinning.
She married that boy there, turned him loose
five confinements later, pastured herself
among the children.

Unlikely little family story,
inappropriate to 1880, mildly
embarrassing, better forgotten, incongruous
with the picture, with the remembered woman
tough as the tortoise she looks like
under her straw hat.

She knew the Scripture she hated, Grandma:
*She girdeth her loins with strength,*
*and maketh strong her arms.*
*She perceiveth that her merchandise is profitable.*
That last is right, at least.

My two girls divided one grandparent
between them, but she was prime.
Besides Grandma Bowers I had two,
something for balance even that early,
when the big ideas were simple: greed
and antagonism, divide, reward, absorb.

How things become artifacts.
The frayed quilt, we took it for ground cloth
because it was past its right use,
the thin batting worn through
in the patches: House in the Woods, beyond
salvation even in that frugal family.
It would sell high, now.

What kinsperson lived at the Pilot's foot,
opened the gate only to picnickers'
quarters, before the state bought
her out? Sister to Cousin Romie's wife
gone strange in her behavior,
so her people set her to guard the gate,
all she was good for?
That name is gone from my brain
like the red clay
I know will wash soon down Pilot's
north slope. Well, I was a child;
what do children notice? How she cringed,
how one blank eye rolled free in its socket,
puffed with what interior vision,
what experience, as she swung
the long gate home.

Later I went there with Girl Scouts,
the surging pontifical leader learned, oracular:
  *you can't eat doughnuts and climb mountains*
  *at the same time, not and hope*
  *to keep your breathing regular, Scouts,*
then with that Arab cardiologist,
sight-seeing, and I kept saying
"No, Muhsin, no, we can't do that
or anything like it on state property."

And yet later my daughters and I picked up
from that same spot
garnets, industrial grade, jutting
from lumps of mica schist, nodes
insistent in their innuendo,
embedded and protuberant as clitorides.

All those generations, birds
in the trees, slate colors, sky,
mountain, rain in a constant slant:
I wonder who's picnicking now,

wonder who's teaching them how;
and Grandma, larded with virtue.
    *Whoso findeth a wife*
    *findeth a good thing,*
but
    *the contentions of a wife*
    *are a continual dropping.*

The north slope of the Pilot
is under a steady shower, a slant
of rain dim already in the late daylight,
fat cloud emptied to flat stratum
leveling the ridge; and here I stand.

3.

How different it looked this morning.

Morning light here in late February is thin,
easing from the southeast
opposite the visible mountains,
those vestiges of the old range.
Early workdays have the grace
of that light, an infusion of pale rose.
It seems substantial as glycerine,
and in the eyes, somehow,
it is; it fills, it pulses in the eyeball,
fresh and healthy; on the skin
it smooths itself, gentle
as cat fur, palpable, pliant. Alone,
I hear it, harmonious under silence,
a rose murmur shot with gold,
dissipated by whistle-sounding time, but good,
good, when the workday starts.

If there are clouds to the northwest
beyond the mountains,
and to the southeast nothing
all the way to the sun

but the space the light fills,
and it is morning as it was
this morning, then that light
reposes on, that light fixes, things
here at the end of its run, momentarily
and slantwise, against the dark cloudbank,
before the rain comes, before
things turn out of the light.

All things; trees: their bare lines are clear
as filigree, three-dimensional
in that they embrace air,
like the Red Grooms paper sculpture of Gertrude Stein,
but flat to the eye against
the early unilluminated mauve-moleskin-colored
sky. They might be trees
of my imagination, for all the real connection
we'll ever have, whether they are
one mile away, at the crest
of that near hill, or fifty, edging
the mountain ridge.
I see them from my window.
I have never approached them.
But they are in my eyes, etched
on my retinas like the scar left
from daring the straight look
at solar eclipse; on the thin
stretch of my brain cells like shadows
of vaporous Japanese on a Hiroshima wall.
The trees are in my eyes
because they catch the light.

4.

I stand in a box of light, balance
on the balls of my feet, heels elevated,
forearms braced on the high windowsill.
My spine is straight within reason
but tipped forward at an angle,

accommodating the available space.
There should be a name, geometric,
alphabetic, architectural, for the form
we make together, the floor's horizontal,
short diagonal zig of my feet,
straight of my legs and trunk:
not quite z, no functional design,
certainly not the extravagance
of cantilever. I lean my face close
to the glass and the rainy late day.
By a trick of light and optics, I see
in the office window with its Mylar glare shield
myself half-doubled, a two-image face
seriously distorted, two noses
with matched humps, three eyes—the center eye
an amalgam, an eye of Plato, a paradigm,
neither left nor right, lashed symmetrically
like a child's drawing. I blink and pull
myself back into myself. The images merge,
the third eye swims into distance, out of my range.

5.

To west and north, all my peripheries—
car lots, water tower, nearby shaded streets,
malls, suburban business parks,
intrusive bedroom communities,
tobacco fields and barns, Sauratown,
trace of the gatekeeper's hut,
even the Pilot's knob,
are gone in the rain, with the day.
The pinnacle like a nubbin
nudged the cloud's mass, cloud enveloped pinnacle
and moved, full, heavy, gradual, down
the plateau toward my bell tower, emptying
itself just as the day poured out all
its available light as my view and I
turned out of it. Dusk, in February,
with rain approaching, and I can go home.

One flip of a toggle switch
and the box I stand in is dark, the windows
merely reflective. An umbrella
open like a long bat wing, like anything
reptilian and prehistoric, is my shield;
I was smart to bring it this morning.
I make my walk home, past parked cars,
past the homes of others, their windows
blind, or squares of light, or vacant.

Rain clatters at the umbrella's stretched silk,
and the ghosts of antecedents,
rackety vestiges, hammer
at my dura mater, for notice,
barely beyond the ear's tympanum.
While I live, they live, I suppose:
demented cousin, silly old loves
and likings, Scout leader; the weeping
old man my father, arrogant
young man my father, who got
what he thought he wanted; his displaced
father I never knew, he never spoke of;
hunkering fat shell my father's mother
as I knew her, the young woman
she was, headstrong. She who ordains:
the conserver. Like her or not.

My daughters have outgrown me.

*When he marked out the foundations of the earth,*
*then I was by him, as a master workman;*
*and I was daily his delight,*
   *rejoicing always before him,*
   *rejoicing in his habitable earth;*
*and my delight was with the sons of men.*

No matter how I crane, I cannot see
the mountain I know is there. The rain is on me.

64